A HISTORY OF BRITAIN IN...

Bites of Food

PAUL ROCKETT

W

FRANKLIN WATTS

Franklin Watts
First published in paperback in 2018 by
Franklin Watts

Copyright © Franklin Watts 2015

Editor: Sarah Peutrill
Design and illustration: Mark Ruffle
www.rufflebrothers.com

Dewey number: 394.1'2'0941
ISBN: 978 1 4451 3609 7
Library ebook: 978 1 4451 3610 3

Printed in China

Franklin Watts
An imprint of
Hachette Children's Group
Part of The Watts Publishing Group
Carmelite House
50 Victoria Embankment
London EC4Y 0DZ

An Hachette UK Company
www.hachette.co.uk

www.franklinwatts.co.uk

Picture credits:
Abomb Industries Design/istockphoto: 17cr; Kseniya Abramova/Dreamstime: 29br; Advertising Archives: 26c; Greg Amptman/Dreamstime: 21cl; Anthro/Dreamstime: 9cr; Artsey/Dreamstime: 13c; The author: front cover br, 25t, 25cl; British Library/CC. Wikimedia Commons: 12, 14b; Cheshire West Museums: 8r; Gaius Cornelius/Somerset County Museum/CC. Wikimedia Commons: 7br; Paul Cowan/Dreamstime: 27cl; Brett Critchley/Dreamstime: front cover bc, 27br; Christopher Elwell/Dreamstime: 19cr; Mary Evans PL: 21bl; flutophilus/istockphoto: 6; Angelo Gilardelli/Dreamstime: 25ba; Global P/istockphoto: 9cl; Joseph Gough/Dreamstime: 5cl, 19cl; David Hanlon/Dreamstime: 4b; Hatfield House/CC. Wikimedia Commons: front cover cl, 16c; HIP/Alamy: 14c; Hulton Archive/Getty Images: 23b; Peter Isotalo/CC. Wikimedia Commons: 15b; IWM/Getty Images: 24t; Johnfoto/Dreamstime: front cover cb, 21cr; Wtold Krasowski/Dreamstime: 26b; Ksena2009/Dreamstime: 7bl; London Fire Brigade/Mary Evans PL: 18c; mamadela/istockphoto: 7c; Nicola Margaret/istockphoto: 23t; Mcxas/Dreamstime: 11br; Monkey Business Images/Dreamstime: 27cr; Alexander Mychko/Dreamstime: 5br; Nevinates/Dreamstime: 8bl; Okea/Dreamstime: 11bl; Lauri Patterson/istockphoto: front cover bl, 29cl; Alexander Piaddet/Dreamstime: 17b, 25ba; Pictorial Press/Alamy: 20; Pixelspieler/Shutterstock: 11c; Norman Pogson/Dreamstime: 5tr; The Print Collector/Alamy: 10; Viktorija Puke/Dreamstime: front cover cr, 13b; N Redmond/istockphoto: 17cl; Sergey Rusakov/Dreamstime: front cover t, 9b; Sanse293/Dreamstime: 16bl; skynesher/istockphoto: 28b; skypixel/Dreamstime: 28c; Stocktrek Images/Alamy: 25cr; Tsekhmister/istockphoto: 15tl; Igor Usatyuk/Dreamstime: 15tr; James Watts/Dreamstime: 29cr; Wellcome Library, London: 22c, 22b; Edward Westmacott/Dreamstime: 4t, 24b; CC. Wikimedia Commons: 18b, 19b, 21br.

Every attempt has been made to clear copyright. Should there be any inadvertent omission please apply to the publisher for rectification.

CONTENTS

BRITAIN AND FOOD

Food can provide a sense of place, history and identity. Just as people like to visit famous landmarks when they travel to places, they also like to try the local food. Many different parts of Britain have foods that are important to their heritage – they provide links to their past.

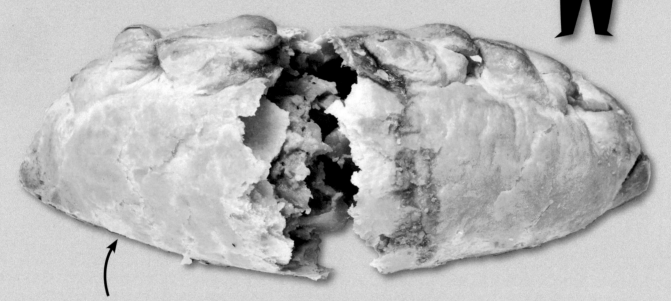

The Cornish pasty is an important part of Cornwall's heritage. It is connected to the local history of tin mining. The pasty could be taken down the mines and eaten without the need for cutlery or plates.

Origins of British food

The history of Britain is one of foreign invasions, wars and empire. Because of this, much of the food we think of as British may not be truly British in origin, but contain ingredients or be influenced by food from abroad.

We may think of the British 'cuppa', a mug of tea, as being British, but it has a history that connects it to India and the Caribbean (see page 20).

National dishes

Britain is a nation made up of the countries of England, Scotland and Wales. These have not always been united as one nation, and each country has their own national identity, of which food plays a part.

Haggis

Sheep's heart, liver and lungs with onions, oatmeal, suet and spices stuffed in the lining of an animal's stomach. Simmer in a pan of water for three hours.

Sunday roast

Roasted meat, potatoes, boiled vegetables, Yorkshire pudding and gravy.

Welsh rarebit

Melted cheese poured over slices of toast, smeared with mustard.

The following bites of food...

The following 12 foods have been part of people's lives in Britain's history. They may be meals that were popular at the time, telling us how people lived or they may be meals that are significant to a particular moment in history. Some of the food may still be familiar today; some may make you feel hungry, some may make you feel glad that they're part of history and not part of your lunch!

FINDING FOOD AT SKARA BRAE

Skara Brae on the mainland of Orkney is the best-preserved Neolithic settlement in Britain. Archaeologists believe it was inhabited between 3200 BCE and 2200 BCE. What we can see there today tells us a lot about how people used to live and what they ate.

Discoveries

The homes that have been uncovered have a main living area with a central fireplace. This was a source of light and warmth and was used for cooking. Around the fireplace are many stone-built containers and a structure, not unlike a cupboard, where precious items, food or tools may have been kept.

Orkney

Storage unit

Central fireplace

Fish tank

Skara Brae is older than Stonehenge and the Great Pyramids of Egypt.

1

Famine food

Limpet shells were found in the homes at Skara Brae. It's thought that limpets were mainly used as bait for catching fish. However, limpets are also known as 'famine food' as they were eaten when harvests were poor and all other food was scarce.

Limpets are quite tough and chewy to eat and were soaked in fish tanks to soften them up. They may then have been heated on a stone over the fire or boiled in a clay pot, causing the meat of the limpet to fall away from the shell.

Limpets are found on rocks near the sea. They are still eaten today, often added to fish stews.

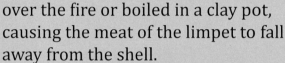

Food facts

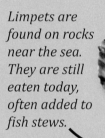

Before farming, people survived as hunter-gatherers. They foraged for nuts and berries in the forests and hunted down animals to eat.

Hazelnuts have been growing in Britain since at least 7000 BCE.

During the Iron Age people started to make metal pots and pans, and tools that made farming and preparing meat a lot quicker and easier.

This is an iron sickle that was found buried on Ham Hill, Somerset. It was used for cutting down corn.

FOREIGN FOOD

When the Romans invaded and settled in Britain, they brought with them many new types of food. These included dates, cucumbers and figs, and meat, such as rabbit and peacock. These expanded the British diet and many are still eaten in Britain today.

Roman banquets

For the Romans, food was a display of wealth and power. Banquets were held to impress guests with unusual and elaborate food, such as peacocks' brains and flamingoes' tongues.

Wealthy Romans ate their food lying on stone benches, leaning on their left elbows while picking up food with their fingers. Slaves served the food and brought bowls of water for the guests to wash their fingers in.

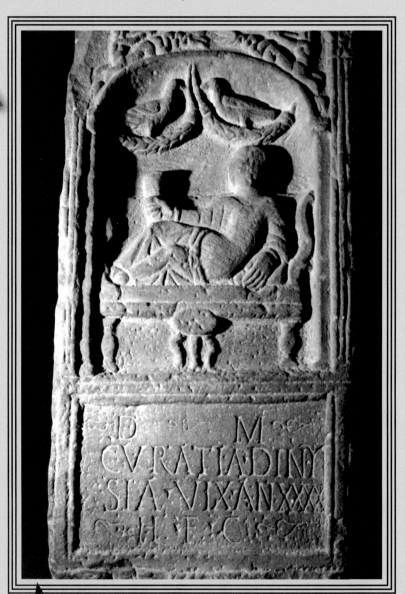

This Roman tombstone was found in Chester and shows a woman enjoying a Roman banquet in the after-life.

The Romans liked rich flavours and brought exotic spices from all over the Roman Empire. They imported cinnamon from Egypt.

Dormice

2

A popular Roman dish was cooked dormouse. Dormice were kept in jars and fattened on acorns.

One recipe has them cut open and stuffed with minced pork or the meat of other dormice. The meat was chopped up with herbs, pepper and pine nuts. The dormouse was then sewn up and baked in an oven.

Dormouse meat has a taste similar to that of rabbit.

Food facts

Poor people ate very simple food. They survived on bread, porridge and a sort of vegetable soup with lentils, turnips, onions and beans. They rarely ate meat.

The Romans brought over wine in large pots called amphorae. Wine was used for cooking as well as drinking.

The Romans made Colchester their capital city, calling it Camulodunum. It's a place that is famous for its oysters – food that the Romans loved. Huge piles of oyster shells dating back to Roman times have been found around this area.

KING ALFRED BURNS THE CAKES

Anglo-Saxon king of Wessex, Alfred the Great, faced many Viking attacks. During a Viking attack in 878, Alfred was forced to hide out in Somerset, swapping his usual royal feasts of meat, for the peasant diet of vegetables and oats.

King Alfred

A story tells how, in Somerset, Alfred took lodgings in a peasant woman's hut.

The woman, unaware that Alfred was king, told him to mind the cakes cooking on a griddle. Alfred let his thoughts wander to his troubles in battle. His absent mindedness caused the cakes to burn and the peasant woman gave the king a good telling off for his carelessness.

The story is told to highlight Alfred as a humble and good king who chose not to reveal his royal identity and claim himself as being any more deserving a person than the peasant woman. It is also a story about the dangers of distraction. Later, Alfred regained his focus and returned to fight the Vikings, beating them in battle.

This is an illustration from a Victorian retelling of the story of Alfred.

3

Griddle cakes

The cakes the peasant woman cooked were not the sponge cakes that we are familiar with today, but more like oatcakes. Griddle cakes were made from oatmeal, some pig fat and a pinch of salt. These ingredients were made into a dough with water, then cooked on a heated griddle stone.

Griddle cakes were a cheap, simple alternative to bread and a staple part of a poor family's diet.

Food facts

The word 'spoon' has its origin at this time, derived from the Saxon *spon* for a wooden spatula.

A cheap and popular dish was pottage. This was a stew of cereals, pulses and vegetables, cooked in a pot over an open fire.

Barley was used to make weak beer, which was drunk instead of water. River water was often polluted.

DEATH BY LAMPREY

Norman king Henry I was well known for having a taste for rich food and spent a lot of his time away from England, living in countries where they cooked with exotic spices.

Doctor's warning

Henry's doctors advised him against eating certain dishes to keep him in good health. They recommended that he not eat any lamprey, an eel-like creature popular with the wealthy.

However, Henry was very fond of lampreys and ignored their advice. He feasted on a large quantity of them, which proved too rich for his stomach, making him violently ill. Within a week he was dead.

Henricus primus

This portrait of Henry I shows him holding aloft his kingdom. Henry ruled England from 1100–1135.

Henry was also Duke of Normandy, a region in the north of France.

Normandy

4

Lampreys

The lamprey has a mouth like a suction pad with teeth that attach themselves to creatures, sucking out their blood.

During the period of Norman rule, lampreys were caught and drowned in red wine, then roasted in the wine that had killed them. They are quite meaty with a taste that has been described as a cross between pork and mackerel.

Food facts

Onion and garlic were rubbed into joints of meat. Meat was hard to preserve and so this was a way of masking the smell and taste of rotting meat.

Today the lamprey is rarely eaten and is a protected species in Britain.

The poor ate bread made from barley and rye, making it dark and heavy. When grain was in short supply, ground acorns were added.

The colour of the bread you ate showed how wealthy you were. White bread was eaten by the rich, whereas dark rye bread, like this piece, was cheap and eaten by the poor.

REVOLTING PEASANTS AND A FEASTING COURT

In 1381, an army of peasants marched into London and captured the Tower of London. They were angry at having to pay high taxes when they were struggling to pay for food. The king, Richard II, had no such problems. He led a decadent lifestyle, and held huge, grand feasts for the wealthy.

Meat feasts

Only the rich could afford to eat meat, and it was the main part of all royal feasts.

A large feast, held in 1387 to honour Richard II, had dishes containing the following list of animals:

16 oxen
120 sheep's heads
120 sheep carcasses
12 boars
140 pigs
1,200 pigeons
400 rabbits
12 cranes
50 swans
210 geese
720 hens
6 goats

Richard II was ten years old when he became king in 1377. In this portrait, he is surrounded by gold to show his importance and wealth.

This image shows a cook preparing a feast with a knife as long as his arm.

5

A cockentrice

As well as dining on sheep, ox and deer, the rich also ate cockentrice. The cockentrice was a dish created by sewing together half a piglet and a capon (a rooster). It was cooked on a spit and coloured with egg and saffron to give it a golden appearance. This was a grand display of invention and wealth.

An artist's impression of how a cockentrice might have looked.

Food facts

Richard II introduced the use of napkins for dining at the royal court.

King Richard II commissioned one of the earliest known cookery books in the English language, *The Forme of Cury* (meaning 'forms of cooking'). It contains around 200 recipes, including one for cockentrice.

Bread was a large part of the peasant diet. As bread was so important, there were Bread Laws introduced to make sure that bakers didn't sell loaves that were under a certain weight.

This illustration shows a baker being punished for selling a faulty loaf. The loaf has been tied round his neck as he is dragged through the streets by a horse.

FOUR AND TWENTY BLACKBIRDS

Tudor explorers sailed out to the Americas, bringing back with them new foods, such as the tomato, potato and sugar. The rich went crazy for sugar; it was a status symbol of great wealth.

Sweet tooth

Grand banquets featured sugar sculptures made to look like galleons and stags.

Vegetables were coated in sugar and fruit shapes were made from marzipan. These were served upon sugar plates which guests also ate.

Queen Elizabeth I was so fond of sugar that it's believed to have rotted her teeth.

Queen Elizabeth I ruled England from 1558–1603. Her mouth is always closed in portraits so as not to show her black teeth.

Those who couldn't afford sugar used honey to sweeten their food.

6

Blackbirds baked in a pie

As well as having musicians and actors entertain guests during banquets, food was also part of the entertainment.

The nursery rhyme 'Sing a Song of Sixpence' refers to the Tudor practice of putting live birds in a pie dish and covering it with a pastry crust. The pie was then presented to guests, cut open and, to shrieks of surprise and amusement, the birds flew out. Live frogs were also used instead of birds.

Sing a Song of Sixpence

A pocket full of rye

Four and twenty blackbirds,
Baked in a pie

When the pie was opened,
The birds began to sing;
Wasn't that a dainty dish,
To set before the king?

Food facts

The rich ate a lot of meat, including boar and swan. When the poor were able to afford meat, they had the cheaper cuts, such as mutton, tough meat from adult sheep.

The tomato, brought over from the Americas, was also known as a love apple. Many people were not sure of whether it was good for you, fearing that it was poisonous.

The potato was introduced into England in the late 1500s. However it didn't become part of the English diet until over 100 years later.

FIRE ON PUDDING LANE

By the 17th century, London had become a centre for luxury food, with large food markets. Many of its streets are named after food that was sold there, such as Fish Street and Pie Corner. Pudding Lane is named after animals' 'puddings' – this is the medieval word for guts and entrails. Pudding Lane is also where the Great Fire of London began.

The Great Fire

The Great Fire lasted for four days in September 1666. This illustration was drawn four years after the event.

The Great Fire started in a bakery and quickly spread across London. Samuel Pepys wrote about the fire in his diary. In describing the destruction, he wrote that:

"The churches, houses, and all on fire and flaming at once; and a horrid noise the flames made, and the cracking of houses at their ruin."

Pepys was concerned about the fire spreading towards his house so he buried his valuable foreign wines and Parmesan cheese in his garden to keep them safe.

Samuel Pepys

Meat pudding

7

The muslin cloth was invented in the 17th century and was used for cooking puddings. The inside of the cloth was lined with flour and animal fat (suet) and filled with animals' guts and entrails. This thickened together when plunged into boiling water.

These puddings became incredibly popular and gained a reputation abroad. A French visitor is noted to have remarked, "*Ah, what an excellent thing is an English pudding!*"

The use of muslin cloth in cooking led to boiled puddings and an early version of the Christmas pudding. Ingredients included spices, plums, suet and bits of meat.

Christmas pudding

A variation of the original meat pudding is the steak and kidney pudding, which has established itself as a traditional British dish.

The first coffee house stall in Europe opened in Oxford. It served a dark, bitter Turkish-style brew. Coffee houses became a place to read reports from Parliament and debate the news of the day.

This is the earliest known image of a British coffee house, from 1674. It shows customers arguing, with one throwing coffee into another's face.

FOOD FROM THE EMPIRE

By the 18th century Britain was expanding as an empire, governing countries from all around the world. Food plantations were set up in the new territories, with the most prized crop, sugar, farmed in the West Indies.

Sugar and spice

Slaves were used to work on the sugar plantations. They lived under cruel and harsh conditions, working to create vast wealth for their owners and meet the demand for sugar back in Britain.

Slaves were whipped to make them work harder. The British government abolished the slave trade in 1807 and outlawed slavery in 1833.

Sugar was now widely available for everyone in Britain, and was used in home baking and jam-making. Its main use was to sweeten cups of tea.

Tea came from plantations in India, as did curry spices, and in 1809, Britain's first curry house, named the Hindustanee Coffee House, opened in London.

8

Green turtle soup

Green sea turtles were taken from the West Indian colonies and transported to Britain in water tanks. Their meat was boiled into a soup with Madeira wine, cayenne pepper and lemon pickle. The soup was often served in the turtle's shell.

The dish was so popular that a variation, called mock turtle soup, was created for the poor. This involved the boiling down of a calf's head as a replacement for turtle meat.

The popularity of turtle meat spread throughout Europe. This image shows cooks in France getting ready to cut the head off a turtle.

In 1765, John Montagu, the 4th Earl of Sandwich, is credited with inventing the sandwich. After he asked his servant to bring him meat tucked between two pieces of bread, others began to ask for 'the same as Sandwich', and so the sandwich was named.

Improved cast iron ovens saw a rise in home baking. Cakes were made with lots of butter, cream and eggs. French and Italian confectionery shops also began to appear in the 1760s.

New metal whisks made whipping cream for desserts easier. Cooks could beat in citrus peel, sugar and chocolate to add flavour. In 1747, the first version of the trifle appeared, topped with whipped cream.

Modern-day trifle

SLUMMING IT IN THE CITY

During Queen Victoria's reign, more and more people moved to the growing towns and cities. Here, large factories and ports held the promise of work for the poor. The cities also had unclean living conditions and most people only had access to low quality food and water, often leading to disease and death.

Dining with disease

This illustration shows numerous people all sharing the same room in a city slum.

The cities were filled with overcrowded slums where raw sewage spilled out into the streets.

During this time there were four major outbreaks of cholera across Britain. This was a consequence of drinking unclean water, which could lead to severe diarrhoea and death.

Many children suffered from malnutrition; lacking important vitamins in their diet they contracted diseases such as scurvy and rickets.

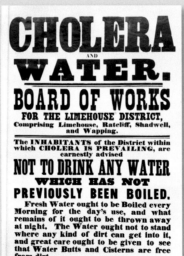

CHOLERA AND WATER.

BOARD OF WORKS

FOR THE LIMEHOUSE DISTRICT,

Comprising Limehouse, Ratcliff, Shadwell, and Wapping.

The INHABITANTS of the District within which CHOLERA IS PREVAILING, are earnestly advised

NOT TO DRINK ANY WATER WHICH HAS NOT PREVIOUSLY BEEN BOILED.

Fresh Water ought to be Boiled every Morning for the day's use, and what remains of it ought to be thrown away at night. The Water ought not to stand where any kind of dirt can get into it, and great care ought to be given to see that Water Butts and Cisterns are free from dirt.

BY ORDER,

THOS. W. RATCLIFF,
CLERK OF THE BOARD.

Board Offices, White Horse Street, 1st August, 1866.

A public notice with advice on avoiding cholera

One of the problems was getting good quality food from the countryside into the cities. An increase in the railway network made this more possible, allowing food such as flour, potatoes and vegetables to travel across the country at great speed and over vast distances.

Fish and chips

Railways meant that fish caught in the North Sea could now travel around Britain within the day and remain fresh. Fish was also very cheap; fried and sold for a penny, it quickly became a popular affordable meal. In the 1860s a stall in London's Smithfield Market served fried fish with chipped potatoes – fish and chips had arrived!

To keep prices down, portions were often wrapped in old newspaper. This stopped in the late 20th century, when it was felt the contact of food with ink was unsafe.

Food facts

Many new gadgets for the kitchen appeared, such as free-standing gas ovens, potato peelers, graters and mincers.

Children buying ice creams from a street seller

Halfpenny ices and penny licks were a small glass that had a scoop of ice cream inside. These were sold by street vendors and proved popular. However, the glasses were banned in 1899, due to concerns over hygiene – the customer licked the glass clean, and it wasn't washed between customers.

THE MINISTRY OF FOOD

During the First and Second World Wars (1914–18; 1939–45) there was great concern over the availability of food. Britain relied heavily on imported foods and the ships that carried them were coming under enemy attack.

Rationing

During both World Wars the government set up the Ministry of Food. The Ministry put strict food rations in place, ensuring that everyone received a fixed amount of certain foods each week.

They gave advice on eating healthily on available foods. This included recipes for rook pie and squirrel soup.

This photo shows a weekly ration from 1942 along with a ration book. The shopper handed over ration coupons as well as payment to the shopkeeper.

A typical weekly ration during the Second World War:

50 grams butter
225 grams sugar
50 grams cheese
100 grams bacon and ham
Meat to the value of one shilling and sixpence
1 fresh egg
1 packet of dried eggs every four weeks
100 grams margarine
3 pints of milk
50 grams tea
100 grams cooking fat
225 grams sugar
350 grams sweets every four weeks

When sweet rationing finally ended in 1953, large queues formed in shops, with people buying toffee apples, boiled sweets and chocolates.

Fake lamb chops

Whereas butter and milk were rationed during the Second World War, potatoes were not. People were encouraged to use them instead of pastry on the top of pies and to add mashed potato to cream to be used for desserts.

Potatoes were also used to create fake lamb chops. Oats, onion and potatoes were mixed together and moulded into the shape of a lamb chop.

Fake lamb chops. Some dishes required a great deal of imagination in the cooking and the eating.

In 1907, the first Chinese restaurant opened in London.

During the Second World War, the Ministry also set up the 'Dig for Victory' campaign. This encouraged the population to grow their own vegetables, setting up allotments in all available garden spaces.

Your own vegetables all the year round . . .

if you

DIG FOR VICTORY NOW

A poster for the 'Dig for Victory' campaign. Even the moat at the Tower of London was used as a vegetable patch.

Lemons and bananas were unavailable during the Second World War because they could not be grown in Britain.

QUICK AND FANCY

From the 1950s, new kitchen appliances speeded up the time it took to prepare and cook food. This gave women more time to do other things. It was especially important as larger numbers of women began to take up work outside the home.

Faster food

From the late 1950s and 60s, many kitchens had fridges and freezers. This meant more food could be stored for longer, so housewives no longer needed to go shopping every day.

A new invention in the 1980s – the microwave oven – made home cooking even quicker. This machine zapped your food with eletromagnetic rays, cooking it within minutes. At the same time, shops began selling ready-cooked meals, which just needed re-heating at home.

This advert from 1955 shows a housewife being presented with a new electric fridge.

Frozen fish fingers went on sale in 1955.

Prawn cocktail

For some, food was seen as a symbol of sophistication, with many of the ready-meals having foreign-sounding names, such as chicken à la king or chicken Kiev. In the 1970s dinner parties became popular and guests sat down to a three-course meal of exotic foods that were meant to impress. Prawn cocktail was a classic starter.

Prawns were presented with lettuce inside a cocktail glass, topped with a mayonnaise-based sauce and a slice of lemon.

Food facts

Britain's first fast-food burger joint, Wimpy, opened in 1954. McDonald's arrived in 1974.

The number of supermarkets grew from just ten in 1947 to 3,400 by 1969.

Fanny Cradock was one of the first TV cooks and a star of the 1950s and 60s. She helped to make pizza popular in Britain.

In 1997, a nationwide opinion poll announced that curry was the nation's favourite food. This has led some to claim it as Britain's national dish.

21st Century
FAST FOOD FATTIES

Fast food is big business in the 21st century and more of it is eaten in Britain than in any other European country. But although burgers, chips, fried chicken and pizzas are tasty, cheap and quick to pick up, eating too much is bad for your health.

Obesity

The popularity of fast foods has led to people becoming overweight. This is because these foods are high in fat and sugar and low in the vitamins and minerals found in fruit and vegetables that our bodies need to stay healthy.

A healthy diet is particularly important for children, as eating too much fast food and sweets can cause ill health later in life.

It's important to have a diet which has less fast food and more fruit and vegetables. It's recommended that you should eat at least five portions of fruit and vegetables a day.

Gourmet burgers

Although beef burgers are originally an American food, they have become a staple part of the British diet.

Many restaurants now serve burgers as their main dish, referring to them as 'gourmet burgers' so that they appear more desirable than those from fast food joints. However, they are also high in fat and so should only be eaten within a wider, healthier diet.

Like most of the food that has come from abroad, the burger has evolved through the tastes and times of Britain to become part of the British diet and of its history.

Food facts

A return to food production of the past has seen an increase in traditional bread baking and cheese making. Home baking, especially of cakes, has become more popular.

Concern over the source of food grew in 2013, when it was uncovered that many supermarket beef burgers were being made from horsemeat instead of beef.

More people have become vegetarian or vegan. Most cafés and restaurants now offer a vegetarian option on their menu, with some just serving vegetarian or vegan food.

More people eat out than they have done before, eating food from sandwich shops, pubs and restaurants. In 2012, it was estimated that people ate out on average 201 times per year.

29

Further information

Books

Britannia: Great Stories from British History by Geraldine McCaughrean (Orion, 2014)
Growing Up in World War Two: Food by Catherine Burch (Franklin Watts, 2009)
The Story of Britain by Mick Manning and Brita Granstrom (Franklin Watts, 2014)
Tracking Down series by Moira Butterfield (Franklin Watts, 2013)

Websites

Information and links to activities on food and shopping during the Second World War:
www.bbc.co.uk/schools/primaryhistory/world_war2/food_and_shopping/

British Library website with interactive artwork leading to facts, audio and transcripts covering the changes in British food over the last century:
www.bl.uk/learning/resources/foodstories/index.html

A history cookbook, providing recipes from all eras of British history with podcasts and fascinating facts about changes in British eating habits:
cookit.e2bn.org/historycookbook/index.php

Find out what children ate during the First World War, their school dinners and food rationing:
http://www.bbc.co.uk/schools/0/ww1/25243103

Activities and games covering different periods of British history:
http://www.nationalarchives.gov.uk/education/sessions-and-resources/?resource-type=games

Note to parents and teachers:
Every effort has been made by the publisher to ensure that these websites contain no inappropriate or offensive material. However, because of the nature of the Internet, it is impossible to guarantee that the content of these sites will not be altered. We strongly advise that Internet access is supervised by a responsible adult.

Glossary

allotment
small piece of land used for growing vegetables

archaeologist
a person who studies human history through physical remains from the past

cholera
a disease caused by swallowing unclean water or food, causing sickness, diarrhoea and sometimes death

confectionery shop
a shop that specialises in selling sweets, biscuits and pastries

decadent
living in luxury with little concern for the well-being of others

empire
a group of countries governed under a single ruler or country

entrails
body organs, such as the intestines, inside a person or animal

famine
an extreme shortage of food from which people may die from starvation or disease

forage
to search for food, such as collecting nuts and berries from a forest

heritage
where you have come from, including items of historical importance and traditions from the past

hygiene
a condition of cleanliness that is healthy

malnutrition
a condition of ill health caused by not eating enough food or enough food that contains important nutrients for a healthy diet

Neolithic
early period of history, also known as the last stage of the Stone Age, when stone tools, pottery and farming developed

offal
internal organs of an animal used as food

origin
the place where something begins or has come from

plantation
a large area of land, especially in tropical countries, where crops such as tea and bananas are grown

pottage
a thick soup or stew made from vegetables and sometimes scraps of meat

preserved
kept safe, prevented from rotting or going bad

rationing
a fixed amount of food given out during a time of food shortage

reign
period of rule by king or queen

rickets
a disease caused by a lack of vitamin D in the body

rural
has features relating to farming or the countryside

scurvy
a disease caused by a lack of vitamin C in the body

slum
overcrowded living area in cities, unfit for living in, but inhabited by the very poor

sophistication
to suggest worldly experience and a superior level of knowledge and culture

status symbol
an activity or object that suggests a person's position in life

Index